MW00777156

KALEY RIVERA THOMPSON

Matrimony Motherhood & Me

TWO MONTHS OF MIRACLES AND MESS

UNITED HOUSE

ISBN: 978-1-952840-11-1

UNITED HOUSE Publishing
Waterford, Michigan
info@unitedhousepublishing.com
www.unitedhousepublishing.com

Cover and interior design: Matt Russell, Marketing Image, mrussell@marketing-image.com

Printed in the United States of America
2021—First Edition

SPECIAL SALES
Most UNITED HOUSE books are available at special quantity discounts when purchased in bulk by corporations, organizations, and special-interest groups. For information, please e-mail orders@unitedhousepublishing.com.

To every married mom everywhere, this is for you.

Table of Contents

Introduction

Dear Mom and Wife,

You are a person. I know it's crazy. But, you are. You are a person with a soul and a calling and a God who loves you so much He appointed you to be a wife and mom.

My entrance into marriage was anything but grand. Three months in and my husband and I were burnt out in ministry and fighting over everything. We quit our jobs and moved across the country with nothing but what fit in our car. Staff housing for our jobs in Aspen, CO was a transformed motel room where we cooked on a hot plate and washed our dishes in a bathroom sink for a year. Honeymoon phase, what?

The beginning of motherhood was just about as movie script worthy. I plummeted into postpartum anxiety after our first child and don't think I felt the release of its constrictions on my mind until after our first daughter turned one. It was dark, hard, and full of sleepless nights and panic attacks.

Somewhere along the way, I stopped asking God to deliver me from my problems and started begging Him to join me in them. "God, if you don't take me there, away from it all, meet me here."

And, He did. Every. Single. Time. I felt like my baby who was learning how to walk. God showed me how to take steps toward a healthy marriage, find my purpose as a mother, and care for my own soul in the process.

If your marriage and motherhood beginnings were far more glamorous than mine, this is for you. And, if they were about as rollercoaster-y, this is for you too.

God's call for us all is to challenge and change the statistics. We can have marriages that last, are exciting, and thriving. We can be mothers who create community, bring life into the world around them, and raise up the next generation of Christian leaders in our country. We can also find time for personal growth and care so we are not running on empty but living out a full life.

I threw in an old term into this devotion book's title. "Matrimony." As in "holy matrimony." Why? Because I want to redefine our modern concept of marriage and call us out of a contract mindset and back into a covenant relationship. I want to remind you of the ancient truths of the Bible that still speak volumes today. And, I want to share with you the lessons I've learned along the wild path of being an imperfect human who has agreed to spend the rest of their life with another imperfect human and then birth and raise other imperfect tiny humans.

In this together,
Kaley Rivera Thompson

ONE

It Isn't "me" It's "We"

"Therefore- what God has joined together, let no one separate."
-Mark 10:9, NIV

Marriage isn't "me," it's "we."

Did you know marriage counselors consider the client the marriage itself? Not the wife. Not the husband. It's therapy for the life built together, not the builders.

It's so easy to focus on what you're building though, isn't it? Look at my beautiful pile of bricks over here that I've laid for us! Check out all I've done! Now, what have you been building? Is my pile bigger than yours? Did you even show up to work today? I think I've laid just a few more bricks than you...

We can move from building a life together to constructing completely separate lives ever so quickly. We're no longer cohabitants of the same relationship, just neighbors watching each other live our different lives.

A marriage is dropping the mortar and laying a lot of grace, forgiveness, and friendship. It's not numbering individual bricks, it's counting mutual blessings. It's taking a sledgehammer to the walls we've built around ourselves and letting each other all of the way in.

If I could go back and add onto my marriage vows it'd be something like this: "I'm excited for whatever life we'll build. It might not be congruent in places. It probably is not going to look like I thought it would. Heck, it could even be constructed out of popsicle sticks or toothpicks in a few areas. But the important thing is it's ours. I want to call that 'home' and open our doors up to everyone we love and throw a big party in it. We're making this life together, and that is worth celebrating."

RESPOND

Do you typically see "Me" or "We" in your marriage relationship?

If you could go back and add something to your marriage vows, what would it be?

Grab some time with your husband and share your add-on with him!

If you could go back and add something on to your marriage vows, what would it be?

TWO

Just Open Your Door

"Do not forget to show hospitality to strangers, for by so doing some people have shown hospitality to angels without knowing it."
-Hebrews 13:12, NIV

If I've learned anything about hospitality, it's this: Just open your door.

It might be messy. One of your kiddos could be crying. You may only have a bag of popcorn and some La Croix. However, when you open your door, you swing wide the opportunity to host angels.

Miracles happen when you share messages on couches. Love gets baked into cookies shared with someone who initially felt hopeless. Laughter over a board game causes all the tension from the week to give way. That person walking through your door might even be the living answer to your prayer.

I'm not going to lie, I love a clean house with a great aesthetic as much as the next gal. Pinterest is awesome, and I have officially Marie Kondo-ed my dresser drawers. However, we can't let the desire to appear put together cause us to close off from community. The reality: There are messy motherhood moments, and it's okay to let people witness, grow, and gain community through them.

Our house might not be perfect, but the love of our Jesus is, and we can offer that freely.

If you've been closed off because of the weight of perfection, just open your door and discover who God might bring over that toy-scattered, crumb-covered welcome mat to lighten your life.

RESPOND

Name a time someone has been an unexpected blessing to you.

Who can you open your door to today?

THREE

Mom grace

"Therefore, there is now no condemnation for those who are in Christ Jesus, because through Christ Jesus the law of the Spirit who gives life has set you free from the law of sin and death."
-Romans 8:2, NIV

Mom guilt is so real.

We are making a million decisions for our kids, which means there are a million ways for guilt to sneak in and tell us we're doing this thing wrong. We're not giving this our best shot. We've failed in this area. We're missing the mark as parents, and our kids are for sure going to end up in therapy.

Here's the truth that's setting me free: Kids aren't looking for perfect parents; they're looking for parents who are perfectly loved.

God is our Father. We're His children. He doesn't expect perfect performance but for us to abide in His grace that covers all our mistakes.

I believe my husband and I are going to disagree, but my kids are going to learn from watching their parents resolve conflict in a healthy way. They are going to discover that eating too much sugar actually gives them a tummy ache, and they probably shouldn't sneak that extra cookie. They are going to see me completely fail as a person and parent, watch God work out great healings in my life and then know He can do that for them too.

Guilt comes from condemnation—when we stick ourselves in the "bad mom" box based on our performance. Freedom comes from redemption—when we admit we are all imperfect at this parenting thing but also perfectly loved by God. It's that guilt-free love we are meant to pass down to our kids.

Is anybody ready to throw in the towel on this mom guilt thing and start throwing out the concept of mom grace more often?

RESPOND

Name an area of motherhood where you've been feeling "mom guilt."

What does it look like for you to extend God's grace to yourself in that area?

Mom

guilt

grace

FOUR

Love your Layers

"(Love) always protects, always trusts, always hopes, always perseveres. Love never fails."
-1 Corinthians 13:7-8a, NIV

When we got married, my husband and I decided to pour sand into a jar instead of lighting a unity candle. We took turns laying layer upon layer of tiny pebbles on top of each other to declare that our lives were so intertwined they'd be as impossible to separate as those tiny sand grains.

Through moving, decor rearranging, and just general passage of time, the layers inside that jar are no longer straight and pretty. They've shifted into each other. They are wavy and out of place. They're imperfect.

Love in all our relationships is like that. Love with God, ourselves, family, friends, and spouses. You start out with this perfect, pristine connection. You pour out your time, energy, and thoughts. Then, life happens— loss, gains, change, babies, highs, and lows— and everything gets shaken up.

However, love is better because of the shaking. Your relationship withstood the fight against cancer. Your spouse held onto hope when you felt helpless. Even when your family felt abandoned, God never left your side.

Take a moment to look at all your lopsided layers. They aren't the mess you saw them as before. They're actually beautiful because they reveal how God always binds messy people together, shaking and sifting makes relationships stronger, and no matter what pushes us down, love never fails to pick us back up again.

RESPOND

Look on the next page and fill in what makes up your layers. Look how far God has brought your relationship! What are the memories that make your marriage beautiful?

How do you look at the mess differently now?

Fill In your Layers

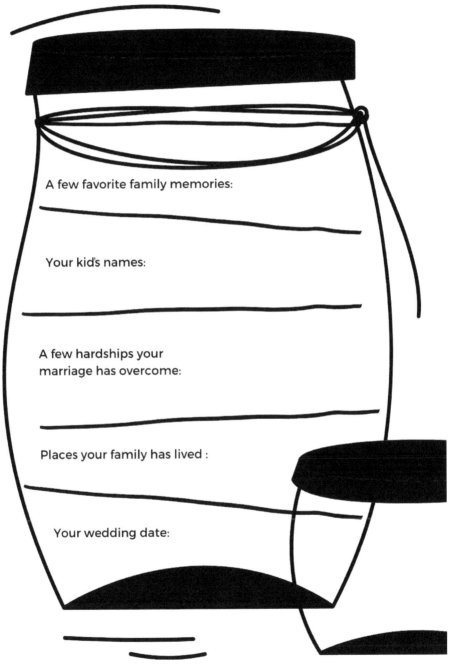

A few favorite family memories:

Your kid's names:

A few hardships your
marriage has overcome:

Places your family has lived :

Your wedding date:

FIVE

The Frontlines

*"Honor her for all that her hands have done, and let
her works bring her praise at the city gate."*
-Proverbs 31:31, NIV

Becoming a wife and mother has not sidelined you.

When I became a mom, I bought into the belief my ministry had been put on pause. I wasn't at "work" on maternity leave, so I wasn't as effectively serving Jesus in my community. Boy, was I wrong.

Here's the truth every wife and mom needs to hear: It is believed that homelessness can be prevented by having authentic community and family or friends who will catch them if they fall. Serving as a wife and mother is a homelessness prevention ministry.

Every time you go to the grocery store, order a pizza, or get baby food smashed into your shirt, you are actually feeding those who cannot afford to feed themselves. Your home is a food bank ministry.

Each moment you listen well to your spouse and create a safe place for them to process or wipe a tear out of your child's eye when something is bothering them, you are serving in the ministry of counseling.

Wives and moms are up to their elbows in hospitality, teaching, philanthropy, sports, and outreach ministries. And, these are just the few we are going to mention here.

You are not sidelined. You were handpicked by God the day you became "Mom" for the front lines. Keep up the hard, holy work of raising children and loving your spouse well. You're changing the world and making a massive impact for the Kingdom.

RESPOND

Have you ever felt sidelined by motherhood or marriage?

How do you see God putting you on the front lines right now?

What "ministry" do you feel most called to in this season of your family's life?

SIX

Motherhood is Servanthood

*"Adam named his wife Eve, because she would become
the mother of all the living."*
-Genesis 3:20, NIV

Mom, I hope you know all you are giving up is giving life.

Dr. Charles Stanley once said, "Motherhood is a great honor and privilege, yet it is also synonymous with servanthood."[1]

Motherhood is servanthood in its purest form. It's God's way of revealing to the world the depth of love it takes to abandon yourself for the sake of someone else's well-being.

Everything you're laying down is raising up the next generation of movers and shakers. All of those sleepless nights, countless hours feeding and cleaning, and moments just holding those babes are not a waste of time but a priceless investment into the timeless Kingdom.

So, rock that messy bun, Mom. Wear that stained shirt proudly. Give yourself the grace God says you deserve. What you are doing with your kids in your home, all those tiny secret moments, those are the big things that are nurturing the world.

RESPOND

Are you honestly giving yourself the grace God says you deserve?

Take time today to sit back and admire your children. The sacrifice it takes to raise them is hard and heavy, but remember, you are doing a great job at this life-giving, holy work.

SEVEN

Strong and Submissive

"Wives, submit yourselves to your own husbands as you do to the Lord. For the husband is the head of the wife as Christ is the head of the church, his body, of which he is the Savior. Now as the church submits to Christ, so also wives should submit to their husbands in everything."
-Ephesians 5:22-24, NIV

Can you be a strong woman and a "submissive" wife?

In my best Christianese, I want to say "yes" because that feels right. "Wives, submit yourselves to your own husbands as you do the Lord..." I mean, the Bible says...

Yet, just the word "submissive" actually makes me want to stick my tongue out and make that "pllphhh" noise because it sounds weak, like I backed down, like I'm one of those pearls-apron-lipstick wearing moms in a 50's vacuum ad.

I'm not. I'm left wondering what strength and submission have in common. Can they truly coexist? Is it possible to bend my will to God's and be a submissive wife?

I did some research and guess what I found out? Being submissive doesn't mean you're a doormat. The Greek word here is "hupotasso,"[2] which means to be under the authority of leadership. It's fully fulfilling the role Eve was given as a helper and fighter.

Submission is strength. They're the same really because it's knowing that the power you hold enables your partner to perform his best as a leader, father, and man. This isn't a power struggle between husband and wife; this is a power share between two leaders. A helper and their help-mate, holding and carrying each other.

You can absolutely be strong and submissive because true submission, to God and man, takes every ounce of strength you have. It's joining forces to let love conquer all. So, husband, I'll give all I've got to fight with you, for you, and for this cause.

RESPOND

What's your insight on being a strong and submissive wife?

Ask God what being submissive looks like for you and your family. If you feel so led, explain to your husband what God has been teaching you about marriage when you hang out with him sometime this week.

EIGHT

A Chocolate Box of Darkness

"You intended to harm me, but God intended it for good to accomplish what is now being done, the saving of many lives."
-Genesis 50:20

God isn't Santa, He's sovereign. However, I really want Him to be Santa.

We all have this tendency to want God to be Santa and give us exactly what we ask. We try to run from situations or circumstances that seem bad or stir up negative emotions. Basically, for me, the rule has been if it's bad, it's Satan, and if it's good, it's God.

The reality is we can feel some negative stuff and be stuck in seemingly impossible circumstances, and it isn't Satan's doing, it's God's.

Poet Mary Oliver perfectly described, "Someone I loved once gave me a box full of darkness. It took me years to understand that this too was a gift."[3]

That's what starting to feel beyond the good has been for me: a giant chocolate box full of darkness. Each emotion offers a different, unexpected, bitter taste. Letting myself be truly angry, broken-hearted, and experience the breadth of negative emotion has been a lot like chewing on a piece of 80% dark cocoa. I note the sharp tang of the first morose morsel and find there's just a hint of sweetness at the end.

It has taken me every day of these last two years to understand the broken heart of postpartum anxiety, the sadness at not being delivered from the pit and the prison when I want to be is all a gift. God is with me here. Even the pit and prison have a purpose for us all.

RESPOND

Name some things that are in your chocolate box of darkness. Take note of the sweet things you're savoring in the midst of a bitter time.

What does it look like for you to trust God's sovereignty today?

NINE

Transactional and Transformational

"Be devoted to one another in love. Honor one another above yourselves."
-Romans 12:10, NIV

Marriage cannot be transactional and transformational.

Seriously, if we're keeping score, we're not counting our blessings.

Things do not balance equally in marriage...or life even. Days go by where parenthood is totally one-sided. There are whole seasons where one person brings in all of the income. Somebody is better at chores, and somebody remembers to pay the bills. I mean, relationships are all over the place.

The biggest game-changer was when I stopped weighing things against my husband and started trying to outdo him in service and honor. I stopped thinking responsibilities and romance was supposed to be split 50/50 and started realizing we were both giving 100%, whatever that looked like for us.

Listen, when a marriage goes from a scoreboard against one another to a springboard for loving each other better, it launches your relationship in a much better direction.

RESPOND

Have you been keeping score in your relationship?

What does it look like for you to stop tallying against your spouse and start trying to outdo them in respect and honor?

TEN

You're a Mother

"For though the righteous fall seven times, they rise again..."
-Proverbs 24:16

Failed? Failed!!!!

The nurse couldn't be serious. I'd never failed anything in my life, and there I sat, in the doctor's office, being told I failed my first glucose test. My reward? I had to go back for another test that involved more sugar, finger pricks, and hours in the doctor's office. Great. Failing is always the worst.

Maybe, like me, you failed your first glucose test. Or, possibly you're dealing with another difficult test in life or motherhood.

There are so many things in this season that seem to slap the "failure" label across our foreheads. But—what if we've been mislabeling ourselves? What if "failure" isn't the negative word we think it is? Failing is really evidence that we tried in the first place.

We are not on the sidelines. We are out here on the front lines giving this motherhood thing our best shot. Of course, we're going to take some hits. We're going to fall on our faces. However, that doesn't mean we're a failure. It actually means we're a doer, a mover, a shaker...a mother.

If you feel like you are failing in some area of motherhood, look at your situation from a different angle. There might be some miracles hidden in those messy moments. Those hits may make you stronger. God will bless your best effort even in the worst situation.

Relabel yourself because you're not a failure. You're a mother.

RESPOND

What words have you let label you in this season?

Flip through the Bible and find some of the empowering words God speaks over you. Start answering to those titles and those titles only.

ELEVEN

Let's Be Dreamers

"Commit to the Lord whatever you do,
and he will establish your plans."
-Proverbs 16:3, NIV

I'm ready to dream again.

Growing up, I had huge dreams. To become a singer/songwriter or an actress. Some kind of sing/act/write triple threat.

Truthfully, I don't know where all that ambition went. At some point, it just dissolved. Moves...marriage...motherhood. Who knows? Has that ever happened to you? What causes this?

Is it becoming a boring adult? All it takes is watching your kids for five minutes to know that children innately know how to dream and use their imaginations. They easily transform their world into another, believe they can be anything they want when they get older, and think they can literally do anything.

We get older and become "realistic," but I'm just not sure we were meant to be so real. We worship a God who gave us those dreams and desires. He can do the impossible, bring life out of dead dreams, and create a miracle in the most mundane moment.

So, I'm going to let the ability to dream big burn in me again, and I'm reminding you to let your light shine if you've lost it.

Let's be dreamers! Imagine all God could do with us if we just gave in to the notion that the impossible, the miracle, could start with us.

RESPOND

Write down three personal goals or dreams that you let dissolve.

Pray today God would breathe new life into them. What do they look like now?

TWELVE

Rise Up Fighter

"I have told you these things, so that in me you may have peace. In this world you will have trouble. But take heart! I have overcome the world."
-John 16:33, NIV

My husband is into what we call "bro sports." Wakeboarding, mountain biking, snowboarding, boxing...stuff the bros like to do. So, when I came to him crying one morning after battling through another sleepless, anxious night, he started to coach me as any good bro-sports enthusiast would.

"Listen, Kaley. You just keep letting your insomnia and anxiety hit you in the face. Quit taking it. When are you going to hit back?"

The fighter in me, who had seemed to vanish through the first year of motherhood, all of the sudden rose up. For a moment, I felt like my old self. Fearless. Brave. Courageously curious.

How do I get back to her? What can we do to fight back against the fear and exhaustion that plagues our lives and robs us of ourselves?

I've never been a boxer, but from what I understand, you not only have to hit back, but you have to anticipate, guard your face, protect yourself, and be one step ahead of the opposition.

Biblically, there are three ways we can do this:
1. Pray with audacity, knocking relentlessly on God's door until He gives us what we need. (Matthew 7:7)

2. Dismiss Satan's lies with God's truth. (Philippians 4:8)
3. Fight from victory not for victory. We are on God's team and know the end of the story. We get the K.O., belt, trophy, and heaven. (John 16:33)

Rise up fighter. You've been hit hard. You have scars and bruises. But, don't tap out. You are not only going to make it, you are going to beat it. Stay in the game. Just keep swinging.

RESPOND

What area of your life do you want to tap out of?

What does it look like for you to hit back and allow God to fight for you when you are too weak?

Get your spouse plus a few close friends on your team and allow them to coach you through when things get tough.

THIRTEEN

Handle It

*"Now faith is confidence in what we hope
for and assurance about what we do not see."*
-Hebrews 11:1, NIV

Can I be purely honest here? I did not know if I could handle having a second baby.

However, we wanted the gift of another child, and I knew if God let us get pregnant again, He'd see us through it. I was rocked with postpartum anxiety and depression after our first child, so I begged God to keep the dark clouds completely away this time. The word that kept coming to me was "help." God, please help me enjoy this gift of pregnancy and motherhood.

Several friends, who have walked this journey with me, have asked, "How did you know when you were ready to have your second baby?" My answer: You are never truly, totally ready for any child. I think sometimes when we're asking God, "What do I do? When do we do this?" He looks back at us and says, "Whatever and whenever. Seek me first, and I'll bless everything that follows."

I'm not saying we do whatever we want but that we make a choice that aligns with whatever God wants for us. We don't have to know if we can handle it; we just have to know that He can.

Even in the hardest of times, God is always helping and holding us.

RESPOND

What do you want out of your marriage, motherhood, and personal life?

What do you think God wants for you?

Search for Biblical truth, and if your desires line up with God's, keep moving forward. I know it's narrow and hard, but you're on the right path!

It's Berry Early
MORNING MUFFINS

Prep Time	Cook Time	Servings
10 mins	20 mins	12 muffins

6 a.m., really? Apparently that's what both of my children's internal alarm clocks were set for this morning. Well, happy day to me. To pass the extra hour of "play time," we made muffins. So, here's the super easy, healthy recipe for our It's Berry Early Morning Muffins. I hope you and your family enjoy every berry early morning that may come your way.

Ingredients

1 1/2 cups all purpose flour

1 1/2 cups oats

1/2 cup Truvia

2 tsp baking powder

1 tsp vanilla

2 TBS maple syrup

2 eggs

1/2 cup Greek yogurt

1/2 cup almond milk

As many berries as you like

Instructions

1. Preheat oven to 350°F.
2. Add all dry ingredients to mixer, and stir.
3. Add in everything else, and stir until well combined. Should be kind of thick but easy to mix.
4. Pour into muffin pan, and bake for 20 minutes.
5. Let cool for 10 minutes.
6. Serve warm with butter.

FOURTEEN

Be a Part of the Miracle

"And if we know that he hears us—whatever we ask—we know that we have what we asked of him."
-1 John 5:15, NIV

What are you praying for in your marriage?

Unity, health, time to date and talk, and being in tune with each other's needs are usually at the top of my list.

There are so many things we pray for and just as many things we are frustrated about not receiving.

Here's what I've realized: When we pray for circumstances within our control, like character-building blessings in our marriage, God doesn't just give us answers. He allows us to grow into our gifts.

God isn't a genie, He's a gentleman. He's going to open doors for us, not force us through them.

Look today for answers to prayer in the form of opportunity. Take that next step in planning a date night or meeting one of your spouse's needs. Speak their love language well. Give them a gift and expect nothing in return.

We get out of our prayer life and relationships the effort we put into them. God loves you enough to let you be a part of the miracle you want in your marriage, not just a recipient. So, get out there. Take all the opportunities you can to grow into whatever gifts you want to receive.

RESPOND

What have you been praying for in your marriage?

What does it look like for you to hit back and allow God to fight for you Write down your requests and let God know all about them. Then, look for answers as opportunities present themselves.

What can you do today to become a part of an answered prayer?

FIFTEEN

What you Expect, you Experience

"...whatever is true, whatever is noble, whatever is right, whatever is pure, whatever is lovely, whatever is admirable-- if anything is excellent or praiseworthy..."
-Philippians 4:8, NIV

Have you ever heard of the term "self-fulfilling prophecy?"

It's the psychological belief that we can prophesy things over ourselves or others and, because of behavioral and mental reinforcement, we cause them to come true.[4]

So, if we dwell on negative thoughts or circumstances instead of the blessings God has in store for us, we can start to become pessimistic about our lives, marriage, and motherhood. We can easily give in to worry or start to think that God's blessing has been lifted off our lives.

But what if we chose to believe God is doing great work for us? What if we took Philippians 4:8 to heart and set our minds firmly on true, noble, pure, awesome things.

Our fear would be overcome by faith. Lies would be trumped with God's truth. Any hopelessness we felt in this season would be overwhelmed by the knowledge of the bright future our family has in Christ.

Know this: what you expect, you experience. Use Philippians 4:8 to prophesy over your family, children, and life. Expect God's blessing. Expect His presence in the midst of your marriage. Expect love and grace to cover your children.

Expect great miracles and watch as they unfold.

RESPOND

Do you tend to expect the best or the worst?

Ask God to help you write down or prophesy some words of blessing and hope over your children, husband, and life.

SIXTEEN

Confession

*"Hear my cry, O God; listen to my prayer. From the ends
of the earth I call to you, I call as my heart grows faint;
lead me to the rock that is higher than I."*
-Psalm 61:1-2, NIV

I have a confession. Remember that beautiful marriage sand jar I talked about at the beginning of this devotional? I broke it.

A few years ago, I asked my husband several times to change out a wreath in our living room but, for some reason or another, he hadn't gotten around to it yet.

"I can do this," I thought, "Who needs him?" I am woman, hear me roar...and watch me climb this really high ladder. In my stubborn determination, I got the broom, climbed the ladder, and swung the old wreath around the handle while tossing the new wreath around the hook. Ta-dah! Everything was a great success until the old wreath slid from the top of the broom handle to the bottom and smacked straight into the jar filled with sand from our wedding day.

Glass shards intermingled with colored sand littered the floor. The only things salvageable were the rocks we had placed on the bottom. They stood for God. They were a symbol of our life and marriage being built upon the Rock.

I love that those rocks were the only things left because they taught me this: the Rock is really all we have. Our relationships, especially our marriages, are going to get shaken up by life, hardship, challenges, and change. Things are going to break— promises, hearts, and expectations. It's going to get messy and sharp and crazy.

The difference is we worship a God who isn't moved or shaken by anything. He never changes and never will. He is the Rock, a firm foundation on which we can all build our lives, relationships, and marriages. God is the only thing left when it all falls apart. He is the same yesterday, today, and forever and ever. Amen.

RESPOND

When life and relationships get messy, what does it mean to you that God isn't shaken by anything?

SEVENTEEN

Thrive and Survive

"The thief comes only to steal and kill and destroy; I have come
that they may have life, and have it to the full."
–John 10:10, NIV

You can thrive in survival mode!!

At least, that's what I keep telling myself and my family. If we can just get past all of the work and church events...When my kids get out of the terrible twos and quit throwing tantrums in Target...Only a few more days until Friday, and my husband will be home to help with the kids...

However, thriving and surviving are not even close to the same. Thriving is living to the fullest, and surviving is just getting by.

So, while you can't actually thrive in survival mode, you can decide to thrive instead of survive.

You can look at your heavy situation and ask God for some great friends to help you carry it. You can make thank you notes instead of to-do lists. You can stop looking at how far you've got to go and start focusing on how far you've come.

In a future-focused culture constantly reminding us of all we've left undone, getting by is our default. It's as if barely making it and being completely exhausted is something to be celebrated. However, when we choose instead to be fully here, present, and grateful for this moment, we find our best selves...living life to the fullest. Thriving.

RESPOND

Do you feel like you're thriving or surviving?

What are some ways to get or keep you out of survival mode and turn your focus toward living out the life God has given you in this season to the fullest?

EIGHTEEN

Baby Clothes

*"A final word: Be strong in the Lord and in his mighty power.
Put on all of God's armor..."*
-Ephesians 6:10-11a, NIV

As we inched closer to our due date, I began washing all of the sweet little baby clothes. Tiny socks. Little shirts. The cutest shoes. I touched each one delicately, imagining the little human that will snuggle into these adorable outfits.

Did you know that, just as we moms begin laying out clothing for our children, God sets out a perfect outfit for them? It's a divine covering that protects them, guides them, and defends them against anything that may rise against them. It guards their hearts, minds, and bodies.

This covering is very expensive but gifted freely from their heavenly Father. It's a family heirloom worn by God Himself and passed down to our children even before they take their first breath.

God is delicately laying out this perfectly fitted outfit for your kids, but it's your responsibility to place it on them, cover them, and teach them how to access its power.

This clothing is armor. It's the armor of God.

RESPOND

Read through Ephesians and use the next page to pray the full armor of God over your children. Incorporate this into a weekly practice. If they're old enough, pray it out loud over them and explain why.

Praying the Armor of God

Lord, I pray that my child/children, _____, will be strong in you and in your mighty power.

Help them to put on Your full armor, so that they can take their stand against anything that comes against them. There is a spiritual battle, a war for their souls, and they need your protection.

I pray Your full armor over _____, so when evil tries to knock them down, they will remain upright and strong in You.

May _____ stand firm then, secure in the Truth of Your Word, their hearts guarded by Your righteousness, and at the ready to tell the world of the Good News. May their faith in You as Defender always go before them, a shield that will deflect every evil scheme. Protect their minds with the reminder of their salvation in You through Jesus Christ. May they fight the good fight with the sharpest weapon ever wielded, the sword of the Spirit, which is the word of God.

**In the powerful name of Jesus,
Amen**

NINETEEN

Be Free

"Then you will know the truth, and the truth will set you free."
-John 8:32, NIV

To train a circus elephant not to run away, they put a chain around its ankle as a baby and strap it to a wooden stake in the ground. As the elephant becomes an adult, it believes it's bound to this position and doesn't move, even though it's now strong enough to break the chain and rip the stake right out of the ground. Its belief in the weight of the chain keeps it in bondage.

Like the circus elephant, most of us enter into marriage and motherhood with some sort of chain. It was probably attached to our lives by doubt or discouragement from an outside source. Maybe we think we're going to be a bad mom. We start to second guess our ability to raise a family or maintain a healthy marriage. We begin to lose our identity in the shifts that this season of life causes. We become linked to these thoughts and allow the enemy to drive them, like stakes, into the foundation of our thoughts.

These chains paralyze us and worry makes us weak. When God calls us to move forward in our faith, we feel stuck.

Here's the reality. You are strong and God is mighty. There's so much power between you both, in fact, that your chains can be broken. You can rip those thoughts right out of your mind. There are no chains on you except for the ones that you allow to remain there.

If your belief in the weight of your chains is keeping you in bondage, allow the knowledge of God's true freedom to start breaking your thought patterns.

You are incredibly equipped and capable of raising a family and placing Christ as the head of your home. You are going to be a great wife and mom because God placed you fully in charge of your life, and when you live it for Him, He helps you see it all through. God designed your body, soul, and mind so it can be restored.

When you feel tied down, recall God's truth. Open His Word and read the promises He has for your family and for you. This is the chain-breaking truth for us all. This is freedom.

RESPOND

Take a moment and identify some lies you have allowed the enemy to stake down into your thought patterns. Cross-reference them with God's Truth. If you have time, write down Bible verses that stand out beside the lies you thought of. Post it somewhere you pass often, like a bathroom mirror or in your Bible, and ask God to allow you to start living chain-free!

TWENTY

Making Room

*"They broke bread in their homes and ate together
with glad and sincere hearts."*
-Acts 2:46b, NIV

What is your family's favorite meal to share?

Family meals are valuable in the Thompson tribe.

There was a whole season of life when Gage and I were newly married and we barely ate dinner together. Our relationship felt tattered and worn and it had only just begun.

After moving across the country, leaving behind our busy jobs and mile-long to-do lists, we found time again to gather. We sipped coffee over breakfast or tried a new dinner recipe. Little by little, we reconnected. To our surprise, we found friends sitting around our tiny studio apartment table too.

Thus began the discovery that food isn't just something we eat. It's really the basis for fellowship.

We no longer have a table for two. In our home, we can comfortably seat five people plus a high chair. We've shoved eight or nine around there on a busy night. It's in that closeness, the messy spaghetti sauce or poured-out pancake syrup, that we really connect. It's nourishing to the body and satisfying to the soul.

That's why we always make room at our table for family meals and for any friends who will join us. Life is richer with connection and community.

A family meal or dinner shared with friends is not about making perfect food. It's really about making time and room at your table and in your life.

RESPOND

Does your family ever do dinner together?

What does it look like to establish this as a priority?

Could you possibly start up a dinner club with family and friends? Once a month, bring in several people you love for fellowship and food around the same table.

It's Pancake Day!
FAMILY & FLAPJACKS

Prep Time	Cook Time	Servings
10 mins	20 mins	10-12 pancakes

Every Saturday, my dad made pancakes for our family. He'd pull out a box of Bisquick, a gallon of milk, (his secret ingredient) vanilla extract, and get to cookin'. It wasn't long before the smell of pancakes and bacon filled the house and roused us from bed. Our family now carries on this tradition by waking up at the start of our weekend and yelling throughout the house "It's Pancake Day!" If you don't have a Pancake Day tradition yet, here's how to start one...

Ingredients

1 1/2 cups all purpose flour
1/2 cups oats
A dash of stevia or 2 TBS of sugar
2 tsp baking powder
1 tsp vanilla

1 cup of almond milk
2 eggs
Any add-ins that you'd like such as chocolate chips, bananas, strawberries, etc.

Instructions

1. Turn your griddle onto 350 degrees.
2. Add all ingredients to mixer, and stir until well combined.
3. Add in wet ingredients, and continue to stir until batter is thick but runny. Gently add add ins after batter is formed.
4, Pour into circles on griddle, and flip after a couple minutes on each side.
5. Stack onto a plate to keep warm.
6. Serve warm with butter and syrup. Take your toppings to the next level with whipped cream or hazelnut spread.

TWENTY-ONE

Educate a Nation

*"Start children off on the way they should go, and even
when they are old they will not turn from it."*
-Proverbs 22:6, NIV

Mothering looks a little different across the world. When I was in Kenya, babies stuck close to their mothers in pouches while they worked in fields. Some women were even considered community mothers or the matriarch of a tribe. It makes sense there's an African proverb that states: "If you educate a woman, you educate a whole nation."[5]

Whether you're in the flatlands of Africa or in a high-rise in an American city, this rings true. Women are mothers who influence not only their children but their friends' children, children's friends, and the whole world around them.

So—what will you do with this awesome opportunity to mold and shape the next generation? What do you want to teach the family and community around you?

Proverbs 22:6 is a promise we can hold fast to as we educate our nation. If we will teach our children what God has taught us, they'll never depart from the Truth.

Let's raise children who know they don't have to be perfect but are perfectly loved. Our children are following in our footsteps, so let's lead those little feet down the path God wants them to go.

RESPOND

Write down three things you want to teach your family, friends, and nation.

Tell God what they are and ask how you can best help raise up the young people around you in the way they should go. What comes to mind?

TWENTY-TWO

True Love Doesn't Have to Wait

"O Lord, You have examined my heart and know everything about me."
-Psalm 139:1, NIV

We're all married here, so, can I be honest?

When I first saw *intimacy* in one of my marriage prep books, it jumped out like a swear word.

I'm a product of the "True Love Waits" generation, and, if I'm honest, I think I basically just learned that sex was bad. As a result, I was terrified for my wedding night and even woke up in a daze two weeks into marriage trying to kick my husband out of my bed. For that delirious moment, I thought we were breaking the rules and forgot he could be that close to me.

I also had some huge mental intimacy issues. I only wanted my husband to know certain things. I believed the lie that if he knew everything about me, if I truly bared my heart, he wouldn't love me the same.

Years later, my husband and I found ourselves in counseling. Nothing crazy was going on, we just needed extra support in a really hard season. Guess what I discovered? My husband could handle my heart. He could see all of my secrets and love me anyway.

Now, marriage is two imperfect people trying to love like a perfect God. It's impossible and messy, which often makes intimacy hard. The important thing is you're figuring it out together.

If your marriage is a safe space for you, here's what I want you to know: You are married! Hallelujah! No more crazy rules and boundaries. God has given you someone who can handle your heart. True love with your spouse doesn't have to wait. True love is here.

So, what are you waiting for? Come out of hiding. Go and unashamedly, intimately love well.

RESPOND

What comes to your mind when you think of the word "intimacy?"

How do you feel that's going between you and your spouse mentally? What about physically?

Bring all of this to light before God and seek to draw your spouse in close. Ask God for help cultivating intimacy in your marriage.

TWENTY-THREE

Dream You

*"'A faithful person will be richly blessed but one eager
to get rich will not go unpunished."*
-Proverbs 28:20, NIV

In my dream world, we own a farm.

We have a giant kitchen with a long table where all of our friends can sit together. We share meals and play board games late into the night. We have a house with spare rooms where people can come and rest and be. It's basically the fall season forever (because, duh), and we have a giant brick fireplace people gather around and our dog snuggles under. There are horses, chickens, trucks, and a giant garden overflowing with fresh flowers and produce. Oh, and a writing shed.

I love the dream world Thompson home (mainly because it's some boho version of a farmhouse that Joanna Gaines would decorate). However, the real world Thompsons don't have most of these things.

Here's the secret: we all have some dream-world version of our lives. We have this tendency to think we can't achieve any of it because it's not our reality.

However, God has actually given us access to what we need in this season to succeed. Start looking at the dream and ask God why that desire is there. If it's from Him, try to interpret the dream into your real world.

For us, that looks like cramming as many people as are willing into our smallish house. We have six chickens in our yard and drive across the street to the greenway to let the girls name the horses that I'm sure already have names. I grow tomatoes and basil in a pot. We don't have a roaring fireplace but we have a pretty great fire pit in the back that people gather around almost every night in the cooler weather.

Proverbs 28:20 tells us to be faithful with what we have and God will bless it. While we may not live in our dream world, we can still bring life to our wildest dreams on this side of heaven by stewarding what we have well.

RESPOND

Dream BIG for your family. Write it all down. Why are those desires there?

Ask God to align your heart for your home with His. Incorporate what sticks from this into your real world.

TWENTY-FOUR

Battle Ground

*"The God of peace will soon crush Satan under your feet.
The grace of our Lord Jesus be with you."*
-Romans 16:20, NIV

I wrote this poem to help you remember that you are an overcomer. You can tell Satan to shove it. Whatever you're fighting for or through today, keep swinging. You've got this because God's got you. Here it goes:

*I'm not afraid of the dark anymore
You don't have to turn on the light
Satan, what you meant for evil
God will only make right.*

*Send me into the valley
Just try to bring me down
One day you'll be cast out
And I'll wear a heavenly crown.*

*You can try to burn me up
But you're only fueling my fire.
When you tried to bring me down
God raised up a fighter.*

*That pit you tried to throw me in
Taught me how to climb out.
That prison you tried to lock me in
Taught me to praise break out.*

I am beauty from ashes
Gold refined in the fire
Thanks for creating the battleground where
God raised up a fighter.

Remember, next time you try to bring me down,
God raised up a fighter.

RESPOND

In God's power and strength, we can and will overcome. Take a moment to reflect on a battle God has already brought you through.

How does that renew your strength to continue fighting today?

TWENTY-FIVE

Serenity

"The Lord will guide you always; he will satisfy your needs in a sun-scorched land and will strengthen your frame. You will be like a well-watered garden, like a spring whose waters never fail."
-Isaiah 58:11, NIV

Have you heard of The Serenity Prayer? It goes like this: "God, grant me the serenity to accept the things I cannot change, the courage to change the things I can, and the wisdom to know the difference."

What most people don't know is the prayer was written by Reinhold Niebuhr in 1937, and there's a second half to it that is commonly left out. It says, "Living one day at a time; Enjoying one moment at a time; Accepting hardships as the pathway to peace; Taking, as He did, this sinful world as it is, not as I would have it; Trusting that He will make all things right if I surrender to His Will; That I may be reasonably happy in this life and supremely happy with Him forever in the next. Amen."[6]

We've been putting too much pressure on ourselves to be content with unwelcome change and hardship within our marriage, family, and selves.

The dissonance and disconnect we're picking up on between the world around us as it is and how we think it should be are unavoidable. We were meant for a haven with God and to live on a fallen earth. We're not going to pray for peace and become instantly cool with the way things are. Why? Because we were made for more. Things are not right.

Serenity is not a passive acceptance of this. It's actively falling in love with God in a fallen world. It's seeing His perfect love all over the imperfection. It's knowing that, while we might be just "reasonably happy with this life," we can still be "supremely happy with Him."

RESPOND

What does "serenity" mean to you?

Write down a few things you find as a source of discontent or things you are "reasonably happy" with right now. How can you find contentment and joy in God in those areas?

TWENTY-SIX

This Is Not A Mess

"He is the one you praise; he is your God, who performed for you those great and awesome wonders you saw with your own eyes."
-Deuteronomy 10:21, NIV

"This is not a mess," I closed my eyes and sighed. My daughter was basically swimming in a sea of toys at this point.

Reality check. It was a total mess. But, it was also a miracle. My toddler was, for the first time, having a blast playing by herself.

Out of the corner of my eye, I caught a glimpse of the clothes all over the kitchen table from the laundry that hadn't been put away and crumbs all over the floor. However, when I shifted my focus from what mess was surrounding me to the miracle in the midst of it all, it changed everything. Instead of feeling like I was failing at "caretaker," I started having fun. All that stress turned into a celebration.

I used to think there was a balance between cleaning and playing, working and family, "mom time" and "me time." Sorry to spoil it for you, but there's not. Life is a juggle, not a balance. It is never a this-or-that choice in motherhood. It's always a decision to do both.

I'll clean sometime...but not right now. Me time can also be mom time (sometimes). And, it's ALL work and ALL play.

So, yes, this is a mess. Life. Toys. Little kids. Big kids. Marriage. Motherhood. However, the fact that God has given us the capacity to juggle is a miracle in and of itself. Let's celebrate that.

RESPOND

When things get messy today, take five seconds and pray God will open your eyes to see the miracle in the middle of it all. Come back and write down what you saw.

TWENTY-SEVEN

Toothpaste

*"Be completely humble and gentle; be patient, bearing with
one another in love. Make every effort to keep the unity
of the Spirit through the bond of peace."*
-Ephesians 4:2-3, NIV

Gage: "Why do you do that?"
Me: "Do what?"
Gage: "Just squeeze the toothpaste wherever?"
Me: "How else do you do it?"
(Gage rakes the toothpaste from the bottom up towards the top of the tube, making it now squeeze-efficient.)
Me: "Ohhhhhh..."

Before I got married, I never even thought about how to squeeze the toothpaste. There are a million other quirky things, big and small, that this relationship has taught me about myself and my husband.

If I was a betting woman, I'd put money on the fact that you're in the same boat in your marriage in some way. So, let's take a moment today to just be grateful for what our differences teach us: How to make tubes of toothpaste squeeze-efficient, that we can respond to the same things in different ways, that God has given us unique gifts we get to offer to the world together.

Unity within relationships isn't the absence of diversity or even difficulty. Unity is making sure division isn't an option.

RESPOND

When things get messy today, take five seconds and pray God will open your eyes to see the miracle in the middle of it all. Come back and write down what you saw.

TWENTY-EIGHT

Living an Answered Prayer

"This is the confidence we have in approaching God: that if we ask anything according to his will, he hears us. And if we know that he hears us—whatever we ask—we know that we have what we asked of him."
-1 John 5:14-15, NIV

It's my first road trip by myself in a while. I'm packing one bag, playing music way too loud with the windows down, and not having to stop to change diapers. It's wild.

The wind in my hair and bare feet on the pedals flashes me back to college road trips, and I realize that this is what I'd prayed for long ago—I'd be on the road with music or ministry. And, here I am, one book and a whole lot of worship rehearsal hours behind me. It's not a full-time gig. It's not exactly what I thought it would look like, but it's an answered prayer.

Don't miss your moment to look into your kid's eyes, feel that wedding band on your finger, let go of that burden, hold up your work, hug a friend, or take a trip and realize that you have unwrapped a gift.

God heard your prayer. Even if it looks different, even if it came at a time you didn't expect it, and even if your spit-up covered shirt is blowing in the wind in your car littered with kids toys and goldfish crumbs while you are jamming out to 90s throwback music.

You hold up that present today and say, "God you heard me. You saw me.

Thank you! I'm living an answered prayer!"

RESPOND

When things get messy today, take five seconds and pray God will open your eyes to see the miracle in the middle of it all. Come back and write down what you saw.

TWENTY-NINE

Sacred Space

"When you reap the harvest of your land, do not reap to the very edges of your field or gather the gleanings of your harvest..."
-Leviticus 23:22a (NIV)

Space is sacred.

So much is vying for our space—kids, spouses, friends, work, and play. Let's not even talk about all the stuff in our home, on our bodies, and around our environment.

I've heard over and over, "Who you are surrounded by is who you'll become." I'd venture to say it's also true what we're surrounded by is what we become.

When we're focused on stuff, we never seem satisfied. When our schedules are too full, we're tired and ineffective. When our house is a mess, our lives seem to follow suit.

I've started to declutter our house, say no to anything that can't go on our schedule, and simplify our stuff so cleaning is easier.

We are desperate for some margin. We need the room. We should be fighting for space in our homes for more people to join us at the table, clean closets so we can see what we have is enough, hearts so God can move, and lives so we see the fun stuff our kids want to do not as an interruption but an opportunity.

Creating sacred space is the practice of enough. Right here is enough. What I have is enough. What we're doing is enough. There's room enough to grow.

RESPOND

Do you feel your family has margin?

What does it look like for you to start creating sacred space in your home and lives? Write a few ideas down.

Do you feel like we need more margin? How do we create more space for rest, fun, and family?

Matrimony, Motherhood, and Me

THIRTY

Satan Cannot Steal Your Joy

"You go before me and follow me. You place your hand of blessing on my head."
-Psalm 139:5, NIV

My husband and I found out we were pregnant the same week we were told our offer was accepted on a house. First baby. First house. It was all so exciting.

But then came a series of unfortunate events. Some things we invested in were stolen. Our car was broken into. My husband got into a car accident. It was as if our joy was crushed by the weight of negativity.

When a woman at church asked me how I was doing, my hormone-raging, sleep-deprived, preggo self was all too happy to unload all of the bad things. There I was, wallowing in my sorrow expecting an "I'm so sorry Honey, let me pray for you" answer. Instead, out came one blunt sentence that redirected my thought pattern for the rest of my motherhood. She said, "Sounds like the Devil is trying to rob you of a blessing."

Oh, isn't he though? Just when God has given you such an incredible gift, wouldn't Satan love nothing more than to make you miss your miracle?

Take your eyes off the burden and zone back in on your blessings. Tune down the lies in your mind and remind yourself of God's Truth. When you are caught up in the little things, talk to a trusted friend or mentor and ask them to give you a big picture of your circumstances.

Satan cannot steal your joy when you've put your life in the palm of God's hand.

RESPOND

What area of your marriage or motherhood do you feel like Satan is trying to rob you of a blessing?

Read Psalm 139:5 again and, as you do, speak it over that situation, family member, or relationship. Let Satan know he can't steal the joy and blessing God has given you.

THIRTY-ONE

Occupation vs. Vocation

"Whatever you do, work at it with all your heart, as working for the Lord, not for human masters..."
-Colossians 3:23, NIV

There is a big difference between vocation and occupation.

Vocation is what we were born to do. It's something that, even if we tried, we couldn't stop doing or pursuing. On the other hand, an occupation is a job. It's just something we do and has nothing to do with who we are.

It's easy to live out our occupations. Punching the clock at a job. Making it through another day of motherhood. Surviving your marriage. But, what if we decided to invest spiritually where we've been just showing up physically? What if we worked not only with our hands but our hearts?

Long car-ride lines could become moments full of potential miracles. Marriage would transform from a contract we signed years ago into a covenant we get to honor daily. Our day-to-day would have an eternal impact. We wouldn't just be working to make a living, we'd be working with our lives.

No matter what you're doing, decide to do it for the Lord. Transform your occupation into your vocation and see what surprises God has waiting for you in your schedule.

RESPOND

What is your vocation?

What would you call your occupation?

What does it look like for you to shift the focus off of what you do and onto doing everything for God?

THIRTY-TWO

Enough

"And God is able to make all grace abound to you, so that always having all sufficiency in everything, you may have an abundance for every good deed..."
-2 Corinthians 9:8, NIV

"Enough" is something I didn't feel I could be as a mom, initially. There was always more laundry. More dishes in the sink. More I could've accomplished as a mother, wife, music director, writer…And then, I read this quote from Oswald Chambers.

"When you do get through to abandonment to God, you will be the most surprised and delighted creature on earth; God has got you absolutely and has given you your life. If you are not there, it is either because of disobedience or a refusal to be simple enough."[7]

We champion the complicated, congested schedules, and lives that are full speed ahead. However, if we really have an eternal perspective, we would slow down in the present. We'd enjoy people, hot tea, road trips, and conversations on front porches. What's the rush? We're actually all immortal souls. We have forever...

Our "rise and grind" mentality isn't the way to create a thriving spirituality. We must be simple in a complicated culture so we can find God in the ordinary, extraordinary ways He tends to do His best work.

Let loving your child, holding your husband's hand, and whatever you have to bring to the table today be enough. Because, when you don't feel like you reach the mark, God promises He's more than enough.

RESPOND

What are some things you can mark off on your to-do list today to create more space for what God wants to do?

It's amazing what happens when we simply give Him our lives instead of our agendas.

THIRTY-THREE

The Best Step

"The man said, 'The woman you put here with me—she gave me some fruit from the tree, and I ate it.' Then the Lord God said to the woman, 'What is this you have done?' The woman said, 'The serpent deceived me, and I ate.'"
-Genesis 2:12-13, NIV

Isn't it so interesting that, from the get-go, we've always been creating distance from each other?

If we time-travel all the way back to the beginning and look at Adam and Eve just after they've disobeyed God and eaten from the tree of life, we see neither of them owns their mistakes or have each other's back.

Adam basically says, "It's her fault."

Eve replies, "The Devil made me do it."

A bit of a rough start for the world's first marriage, right? This theme of creating distance between each other and a lack of ownership over our mistakes have continued on until the present day. It wreaks havoc on our marriages and tears apart families.

If I was having coffee with you right now, and you asked me what is the next step you should take in your marriage, I'd write this down on a napkin and tell you to stick it in your purse to save for later:

In marriage, the best step to take is toward each other.

Stop finger-pointing and start having your spouse's back. Own your mistakes and give your husband a safe space to own his. Move toward each other and you'll find God transforming your marriage issues into opportunities.

RESPOND

When issues arise in your marriage, do you tend to finger point or lock arms with your husband?

What does it look like for you to step toward your spouse in this season?

THIRTY-FOUR

Heavy

"God is within her, she will not fall;
God will help her at break of day."
-Psalm 46:5, NIV

Motherhood is heavy, so let's help each other carry the weight.

There are a million ideologies on how to parent out there. When we belittle or gossip about other mothers because we don't agree with their parenting style, we are basically just adding to their already heavy load. What if we lifted fellow moms up in prayer and encouragement instead?

I just read an article in InStyle magazine that listed suicide as one of the top causes of postpartum deaths in America.[8] Depression and anxiety are at an all-time high for moms across the board.

Let's face it, we need a motherhood revival. It should be our goal to make sure fellow moms don't feel so lonely, overwhelmed, and angry. Let's let friendships flourish between us at playgrounds. Abandon post as an independent fighter, and let's stand as a united front to support our children.

Consider this story. Moms with different opinions were all on the same side of the street. They were fighting about whether or not breastfeeding was best, what food kids should be eating, how to discipline them, what education sets them up for the most success, etc. All of a sudden, an un-attended stroller with a baby inside started to roll down a hill. All of the mothers stopped fighting at once and began chasing after the runaway stroller.

You see, when it comes down to it, it's not making our opinions known that we really want. We are actually all chasing after the same thing—to have happy, healthy, awesome kids. So, let's do it together.

RESPOND

How can you intentionally uplift another mother today?

While you are driving your kids to school or are on a break at work, take time to pray for any moms that come to mind.

THIRTY-FIVE

Stolen

"...but God has surely listened and has heard my prayer."
-Psalm 46:5, NIV

Once upon a time, my husband and I were cool, and we rode motorcycles. I had a rad gold sparkly helmet that, if it was appropriate, I would have worn all of the time because I loved it that much.

To make a long story short, my husband and I decided to sell our bike when we found out we were pregnant and buying a house all in the same week. During the sale, it was stolen. Our down payment on our house was ripped away from us.

I prayed so long for the return of our motorcycle that, in my prayer journal, the request was no longer a sentence. Just a "$" symbol. Just a pining, aching thought.

God hears us when we pray. He speaks even when we think He's silent. He is at work in our lives even when we don't see a single answer budding on the surface.

Two years later, a cop called to inform us our bike was found. As it rumbled its way back into our driveway, I felt like I heard God saying, "Never stop praying. Never doubt for a moment I am at work in every single thing. Never lose faith in the Taker, Giver, and Provider of all things."

Hallelujah! God hears! He may answer in His own timing and way. But, He hears us all.

RESPOND

Do you have any prayers you have given up on?

How can you find fresh inspiration to begin talking to God about it again?

If you feel led, begin praying that old prayer today.

THIRTY-SIX

Stop Looking At That Window

*"I keep my eyes always on the Lord. With him at
my right hand, I will not be shaken."*
-Psalm 16:8, NIV

"I had this window in my house. When my kids were little, all I could think about was how dirty that window was going to get," she said. "Eventually I just had to stop looking at that window. I had to start seeing my kids."

It was the best phone call from a doctor I'd ever received. What started out as a follow-up chat about how my postpartum anxiety medication was working, ended up as amazing advice. Here's what I learned:

Our perspective guides our purpose.

We can focus on messes or miracles. We can be busy or enjoy our blessings. We can proactively live our best life or reactively let life live us. We can either grumble about dirty windows or give God gratitude for little fingerprints.

If we feel disheartened, overwhelmed, or confused, we are probably dwelling on the wrong things and need to fix our focus.

RESPOND

What do you think about the most each day?

Do your thoughts line up with your family's priorities and God's desires for you?

If your answer is no, write down what you believe God wants you to be focusing on.

THIRTY-SEVEN

God Brought You Out

"On that day tell your son, 'I do this because of what the Lord did for me when I came out of Egypt.' This observance will be for you like a sign on your hand and a reminder on your forehead that this law of the Lord is to be on your lips. For the Lord brought you out of Egypt with his mighty hand. You must keep this ordinance at the appointed time year after year."
-Exodus 13:8-10, NIV

I was stuck rereading Exodus 13:8-10 over and over this morning.

The Israelites had just been set free from hundreds of years of slavery in Egypt. Generational prayers were answered. Chains were broken.

Do you want some good news today? This freedom message is for us too because we've all been in slavery to something. Let's break the chains of any addiction, heartache, guilt, condemnation, worry, fear, sin, anxiety, oppression, etc. by reading it like this. You fill in the blank:

"This is what God did for me when I came out of _____.
All I do is guided and empowered by this deliverance.
It was with a powerful hand that God brought me out of _____."

It was with a powerful hand that God brought you out. Did you catch that? GOD BROUGHT YOU OUT!

He has and will do it again. Remember all that God has done for you, choose intentionally to live by that truth, and walk in your deliverance today.

RESPOND

Take time to fill in the blanks on the next page. How does reflecting on all that God has done for you in the past make you feel about your future?

If you need deliverance from something today, tell God what he's done for you before and ask Him to do it again.

This is what God did for me when I came out of

_____

All I do is guided and empowered by this deliverance.

It was with a powerful hand that God brought me out of

_____

God brought me out!

THIRTY-EIGHT

I'm Thankful for...

"Devote yourselves to prayer, being watchful and thankful."
-Colossians 4:2, NIV

"Three Things I'm Thankful For:"

I write that heading in my journal every day. Some days finding those three things comes easy, and other days (when the kids are screaming at me, there's spilled cereal across the table in front of me, and I'm about to reheat my coffee for the third time), it's a bit harder to do.

If you are like me, it's easy to forget to be thankful. Our prayers can easily turn into a "Jesus do" list.

"Jesus, will you do this?"
"God, will you do that, take this, show something, give it.....?"

God is not an errand boy, so we have to take a look at what He has already done. Create pause in your daily life to see what God is up to in your every day.

My top three things aren't always happy-sappy. Coffee tends to frequent the list (even the reheated kind). So does an argument Gage and I had that helped us grow in the long run, how fierce my girls are, and that I live in a house that I get to clean (whew, I'm really stretching for that one, okay).

Thank God for the process.

Thank God for the good and easy.
Thank Him for the laundry.
Thank Him for the grit.

It's all something to be thankful for because both your confetti bursting moments and times spent crying on your pillow mean you are alive, gloriously human, in the midst of a messy miracle, and wonderfully His.

RESPOND

If you typically keep a journal, add writing in three things you're thankful for into your daily reflection time. If not, try thinking of three things every morning while you're getting ready or driving into work.

Use this book or a journal to note any changes thankfulness brings to your interaction with God or perspective on life.

THIRTY-NINE

Super Mom

*"And let us consider how we may spur one another on toward
love and good deeds, not giving up meeting together, as some
are in the habit of doing, but encouraging one another—and
all the more as you see the Day approaching."*
-Hebrews 10:24-25, NIV

I passed a mom in Target today, and she really was (Da-da-da-DAHH!) Super Mom!

She was pushing a double stroller with a baby and toddler inside with one hand and a shopping cart with the other. If that isn't a superpower, I don't know what is.

I passed her coming down an aisle. My girls were fussing while her boys were content as could be. We both made eye contact and, without saying anything, told each other how hard this was.

"You're super mom!" The words fell right out of my mouth.

"No, you are," she replied. I responded with one of those awkward smiles where you are actually blinking back tears.

My heart leapt at her words. All of the sudden, life felt a little lighter. Why? Because encouragement is sharing the burden because it lets us know we are not alone.

In case you needed to hear those words just as much as I did today, I want to speak them over you too. You are a super mom. You are doing this the best you can. God has uniquely equipped you and called you for this mission to care for the children you have specifically been given.

Keep going. There's a team of women around you believing in you and cheering you on.

RESPOND

Pass on the message. Reach out to a fellow mom today and send her some encouragement. Let her know her superpowers, that you see her, and are proud of her.

FORTY

Are you Important?

"For where your treasure is, there your heart will be also."
-Luke 12:34, NIV

Let me ask a question. Are you important to the people you need to be important to?

As a work-from-home mom, I often feel unseen. There's no pat on the back from coworkers to assure me that I'm doing an okay job. There are no conversations in the break room to get me through the day. Sometimes, I just want to stick my head out of the car window while my kids are crying in the back seat and scream, "Hello world!!! Do you see me? Do I matter to you??!!"

Here's the deal. In this season, it's not important what the world thinks of me. However, it is important what my girls, husband, and our ministry think of me.

Maybe you're a mom scrolling through social media looking for some validation or socialization. Possibly you're at your office wondering if you've impressed your boss enough or if you matter enough to your coworkers. You could be planning a date with your husband and not enjoying the process because you're more worried about it looking Instagram-awesome than creating a space where you both can truly connect.

Let go of the desire to be important to people that don't matter and focus your attention on the people that really do. That's really a simple definition of "calling." Our purpose in life is to show up and make a huge impact in our tiny niche.

RESPOND

How would you answer the question, "Are you important to the people you need to be important to?"

What can you do to keep your focus on the things and people that matter most in this season?

FORTY-ONE

Love Is...

"Love is patient, love is kind. It does not envy, it does not boast, it is not proud. It does not dishonor others, it is not self-seeking, it is not easily angered, it keeps no record of wrongs. Love does not delight in evil but rejoices with the truth. It always protects, always trusts, always hopes, always perseveres."
-1 Corinthians 13:4-7, NIV

A lot of us define love by 1 Corinthians 13:4-7. However, this verse isn't just an idea of love. It's actually the way we are to define our lives and characterize our relationships. Why? God is love, and we are to love like Him.

In a nutshell, we should be able to fill our name in the blank. Try it.

_____ is patient, _____ is kind. _____ does not envy, _____ does not boast, _____ is not proud. _____ does not dishonor others, _____ is not self-seeking, _____ is not easily angered,_____ keeps no record of wrongs. _____ does not delight in evil but rejoices with the truth. _____ always protects, always trusts, always hopes, always perseveres.

I can't even begin to fill in one blank without realizing that I struggle with basically every part of Godly Love in some way. When my kids throw Cheerios on the floor…again, I am not patient.

I'm constantly tempted to force my husband to earn respect instead of honoring Him simply for the fact that he is the leader God has appointed for our family. Give me any fight and I instantly can recite a record of wrongs as a comeback.

Here's the deal. God doesn't expect us to love perfectly. Only He can do that. But, He does desire for us to be transformed by the way He perfectly loves us.

There is grace for mistakes in marriage and motherhood. There is a love that covers all sins. So, when we fail at love, God steps in on our behalf and gives us His heart for our family. Our hearts can soften in the fight. We can give our frustration to God and let Him replace it with His patience for the process. He can take the history of our past mistakes and begin to write a new story in our relationships.

Real love is hard. It's serious business. So, let's get serious about love and living loved.

RESPOND

Take a moment to fill in the next page. Which blank or blanks did you struggle to write your name in the most?

Ask God to work on you in that area and reveal how you can love your family, spouse, and others as He does.

Fill in the blank with your name.

_____ is patient.
_____ is kind.
_____ does not envy.
_____ does not boast.
_____ is not proud.
_____ does not dishonor others.
_____ is not self-seeking.
_____ is not easily angered.
_____ keeps no record of wrongs.
_____ does not delight in evil but
rejoices with the truth.
_____ always protects.
always trusts.
always hopes.
always perseveres.

FORTY-TWO

Sweat It

"But David said to Saul, "Your servant has been keeping his father's sheep. When a lion or a bear came and carried off a sheep from the flock, I went after it, struck it and rescued the sheep from its mouth. When it turned on me, I seized it by its hair, struck it and killed it. Your servant has killed both the lion and the bear; this uncircumcised Philistine will be like one of them, because he has defied the armies of the living God. The Lord who rescued me from the paw of the lion and the paw of the bear will rescue me from the hand of this Philistine."
-1 Samuel 17:34-37a, NIV

They say, "Don't sweat the small stuff." I don't know who "They" is but "They" are wrong. I say sweat it. Care a lot about the little things.

When you're tempted to think that tiny moments like playing with your kids on the floor, holding your husband's hand, or relaxing just a little longer in the bathtub don't add up to much, think about these facts: A spark can start a fire, big dreams are accomplished in small steps, and giants are taken down with tiny stones.

Do you know the story of David before he killed Goliath? We don't have time for it all here today, so here's the short of it. He was anointed to be king and then sent back to a sheep pasture for years before he actually rose to power.

Like David, glean every tool and talent you can in the field of mother-hood and marriage. He would have never slain a giant or been invited into the king's palace if he had not learned to use a sling and play the harp in his hidden place. If he would've been annoyed by the fieldwork, he would've missed out on the anointing for his Kingdom work.

What we practice in private will be used in public. Everything we do in secret can be used to save others. These moments of motherhood and marriage may seem small now, but God can do great things with a little faith.

RESPOND

What daily moments seem small but are actually a big deal?

Take time today to zoom in on them, weigh how heavy their impact actually is on your family and marriage, and pray that God will transform your fieldwork into Kingdom work.

FORTY-THREE

The Motherhood you Were Made For

"God blessed them and said to them, "Be fruitful and increase in number; fill the earth and subdue it. Rule over the fish in the sea and the birds in the sky and over every living creature that moves on the ground."
-Genesis 1:28, NIV

Identity crisis is common at the beginning of motherhood. We are "Mom" now. What does that mean? Did we become different people when a babe was placed into our arms? What is our purpose? Who are we meant to be?

A safe way to find out the answer to identity questions is to flip back in the Bible to find out God's creational intent for things. Before sin entered the world, what did God want a mom or woman to be?

Our best clue is Genesis 1:28. In short, it reveals mothers are life bringers, rulers of the earth, and strong protectors of our family. Basically, we're all wonder women, and I can totally get behind that.

God does this really beautiful thing in Genesis where he creates a massive, lavish garden and places Adam and Eve there to cultivate the plants, rule over the animals, and begin the world's first civilization.

While we don't live in Eden anymore, our purpose remains to be mothers over all the living by caring for our own children and raising up those around us in the Love of Christ (Gen. 3:20). We are also still gardeners, planting seeds of hope, truth, and joy into the world in order to let God's purpose flourish.

Are you ready? This is my favorite part about our identity as women and mothers. The word used for man's partner in Genesis 2:18 is "helper," which translates in Hebrew to "ezer," which is some version of "strong rescuer." We are fighters for our families. The term "Mama Bear" is women putting God's strength on full display. We are beside our husbands as rulers of the earth, warriors for the Kingdom, and defenders of life and love.

While we all have our own unique way of mothering, our identity is all found in the same place. We are God's women chosen for the high honor of being called "Mom."

RESPOND

What do you think defines a mom?

How do you identify yourself in this season?

How do you think God has called you to defend, cultivate, and create life in your family and the community around you?

FORTY-FOUR

The Only Way To Win

"When Moses' hands grew tired, they took a stone and put it under him and he sat on it. Aaron and Hur held his hands up—one on one side, one on the other—so that his hands remained steady till sunset. So Joshua overcame the Amalekite army with the sword."
-Exodus 17:12-13, NIV

Find friends who will hold you up when you are tired.

You'll conquer enemies. You'll lead better. You'll take new ground. You'll deliver others.

At least, that's what happened with Moses. When he held up his hands against the Amalekites, the Israelites began to win the battle. When he put them down, the Israelites started to lose. So, Moses got stuck with the awesome job of hand-holder-upper.

When Moses' arms grew tired, his right-hand men (no pun intended), Aaron and Hur, gave him a stone chair and supported him by helping to hold his hands high.

My entrance into motherhood was rough. I was depressed and lost and failing at breastfeeding. It was as if a little gray cloud had settled over my head and expanded throughout my home. I couldn't escape it. I hit a breaking point. And, guess who showed up?

My friends came over to hold my baby when I was too tired. Grandparents gave me space to shower and rest. My husband held my hand through the hardest of nights and released me to do what I needed to do to become mentally healthy. As soon as I let others come in and hold my arms up for me, I began to see a victory. The clouds parted. It was their strength that got me through.

You see, we desperately need others. No woman is an island, and marriage and motherhood are exhausting.

Admit when you're tired and let the strength of others support you. It's the only way to win the fight.

RESPOND

Who is a friend who has helped hold you up when you wanted to tap out?

Reach out to them and thank them today. Ask God if there is someone around you who needs your support? Offer it.

FORTY-FIVE

Noise and News

"For to us a child is born, to us a son is given, and the government will be on his shoulders. And he will be called Wonderful Counselor, Mighty God, Everlasting Father, Prince of Peace."
-Isaiah 9:6, NIV

There's so much noise right now. There's even noise about the noise.

We feel paralyzed because the world seems so bad. What good would anything good actually do? Why would we speak when no one would hear? Why would we spark change if no one will catch fire?

I turned off the news a long time ago. Don't worry, I check in so I can be "relevant." But coming from a public relations background, I know about fear tactics and the "any news is good news" kind of mentality. Despite my heightened awareness, I was tricked into reading the headlines and watching the next feed of biased, negative information.

Here's what I learned: there is one source of Good News. It's called the Bible. There's one person that won't lie. That's God. There's a single, beautiful sound over all that's going on, and that's the song Jesus is singing over it all.

Don't be so bombarded by the noise that your hope is silenced and you miss the voice of Love woven through it all. Don't hold back when you've been sent out into the world to not only talk about the issues but actually make a difference.

Find what you are good at and be good at it for the good of others. Your actions will be the shot heard around the world ringing out that there is good and God is in the midst of it all.

RESPOND

Take a moment to write down or pray about some of your major worries about the world right now. Ask God to rewrite the headlines in your mind, equip you to do good in your community, and remind you that the government rests on his shoulders.

FORTY-SIX

Contentment

*"I am not saying this because I am in need, for I have
learned to be content whatever the circumstances."*
-Philippians 4:11, NIV

I have learned to be content in all things...Hahaha! Just kidding. I have not learned this.

I always want more out of life. Not in a materialistic way, but in an I-want-to-drink-in-life-from-a-fire-hose kind of way. I'm constantly wondering if the grass is greener on the other side, trying to plan what's next on the schedule for my kids, dreaming about the future, and striving to achieve. What I'm really asking is, can I have my cake, my family's cake, some other cake samples, and eat it too?

However, what Paul is sharing in Philippians 4 is the key to contentment I think most of us are missing. After all his life experience, he lands on, "I can do all this through him [Christ] who gives me strength" (Philippians 4:13, NIV).

The "this" he is referring to is contentment. We can't be content on our own. We can't be enlightened to it. We can't just wake up one day and go, "Wow, I'm so perfectly fine with everything that isn't fine in my life." We can't be content without Christ.

We're really doing contentment all wrong. We're forcing ourselves to appreciate what we have when we can be grateful that God thought to give it to us. We're trying to be satisfied with life as it is, but really, we need to be okay with what it isn't. The issues, anger, hurt, and pain may not be fulfilling but they're fulfilling God's purpose for us.

Everything in life doesn't have to be satisfying to be sanctifying.

While we may be weak when it comes to wanting more from life, we can be strong in the God who wants the most for our lives. We can be totally dissatisfied with a place and space and yet completely content with Christ.

RESPOND

What are you most discontent about right now?

What does it look like for you to look at your situation through a different lens and seek contentment in Christ?

FORTY-SEVEN

Cheap Date

"So they are no longer two, but one flesh. Therefore what God has joined together, let no one separate."
-Matthew 19:6, NIV

Sometimes, I wonder if our culture has overcomplicated dating.

There are reservations and plans and really high expectations and stress and nerves.

I'm rebelling. I want dates to be freeing, conversational, fun, and centered around connecting with my spouse.

I want to be a cheap date.

For some reason, the cheap dates always turn out to be the best ones for my husband and me. We pack a picnic, go sit by the lake, and simply be with each other. It costs us nothing, and the time together is absolutely priceless.

There's nothing wrong with fancy dinners in the city, but it can all go wrong when the concern for date night plans and capturing Instagram-perfect pictures exceeds our care for connection with each other.

So, be a cheap date this week. Keep it simple. Let the highlight be engaging with your spouse.

RESPOND

Plan a date. Here's the criteria: It must be very fitting for who you are as a couple, simple, with the main goal to connect and communicate. You have to ask your husband out. Ready? Set. Go!

date night planner

Where?

What?

When?

Babysitter's #:

Reservation time:

Other notes:

- - - - - - - - - - - - - - - ✂

Dear Husband,
I would like to take you on a date. Will you join me on _____ at _____? Be ready because I'm picking you up at _____. I can't wait to see you!

Love,
Your Wife

FORTY-EIGHT

What is That in your Hand?

"Then the LORD said to him, "What is that in your hand?" "A staff," he replied. The LORD said, "Throw it on the ground." Moses threw it on the ground and it became a snake, and he ran from it. Then the LORD said to him, "Reach out your hand and take it by the tail." So Moses reached out and took hold of the snake and it turned back into a staff in his hand. "This," said the LORD, "is so that they may believe that the LORD, the God of their fathers—the God of Abraham, the God of Isaac and the God of Jacob—has appeared to you."
-Exodus 4:2-5, NIV

"What is that in your hand?"

I'm slowly trodding through the Bible and onto Exodus now. In Chapter 4, God is talking to Moses through the burning bush and gives him a HUGE commission to set the Israelites free from slavery in Egypt.

In short, Moses doubts people will believe him when he rolls up and says, "Let my people go." So, God gives him proof to offer the people.

Often, we are waiting on God to assemble some divine tool for us in order to accomplish all He has asked us to do. However, our God is famous for using mundane things to perform miracles. Here are a quick few:

- Jesus used a little boys' lunch box to feed over 5,000 families.

- Jesus wiped mud into a blind man's eyes so he could see.
- God created the bloodline of Christ out of dysfunctional families.
- A cross gave us eternal life.
- God used Moses' walking staff to turn into a snake, transform the Nile into blood, part the Red Sea, and bring water out of a rock.

Let me ask you this question today, "What do you have in your hand?"

Quit waiting for God to give you something else when He's waiting for you to use what you've already been given.

RESPOND

Sit in a quiet space for a moment and evaluate your resources. What do you have in your hand right now?

What do you think God is asking you to do with it?

FORTY-NINE

Who We Are Sets The Bar

*"Listen, my son, to your father's instruction and do not forsake
your mother's teaching. They are a garland to grace your
head and a chain to adorn your neck."*
-Proverbs 1:8-9, NIV

Confession. I stayed up late last night so I could watch Gilmore Girls. Alone.

"Alone" is this deep need we get as parents to just shower, go to the bathroom, drive in the car, curl up on the couch with our favorite cup of hot tea, or anything at all completely by ourselves. LEAVE ME ALONE!

I relished in my alone time by putting on the episode of Gilmore Girls when Rory, one of the main characters, graduates high school. She's a classic overachiever who is awarded valedictorian and has to give a speech on graduation day. She thanks a lot of people, but the person she gives the highest honor is her mother. I bawled.

She talked all about the books and music her mother taught her to love and the historical role models her mom told her to look up to. Rory ends with some version of "What she didn't know was, the person I wanted to be like most was her." Cue the waterworks.

I became painfully aware in that moment that our goal as mothers is not just to raise our children to be God-fearing, positively contributing, wise adults but to actually emulate that for them. Our actions carry further than our words. Who we are sets the bar for who we want our kids to become.

I know Gilmore Girls isn't exactly spiritually edifying. However, this echoes the principle we find in Proverbs 1:8-9. Our children embody our teaching and instruction. Let's be who we want them to become. May our ceiling be their floor.

RESPOND

Write out your kids' names and bullet point a few notes about the potential you see in each of them. How can you live out some of these characteristics for them?

What does it look like for you and your spouse to intentionally be role models for your children?

FIFTY

The Father's House

"The older brother became angry and refused to go in. So his father went out and pleaded with him. But he answered his father, 'Look! All these years I've been slaving for you and never disobeyed your orders. Yet you never gave me even a young goat so I could celebrate with my friends. But when this son of yours who has squandered your property with prostitutes comes home, you kill the fattened calf for him!' "'My son,' the father said, 'you are always with me, and everything I have is yours."
-Luke 15:28-31, NIV

Holding my baby girl, I study her face. I run my fingertips over wisps of soft hair and over tiny pink lips. She looks back at me with stunning blue eyes and I wonder what she's thinking. What big potential is yet to be discovered in that tiny heart?

Stop for a moment and realize that God holds us, His children, like this too. He has studied our stray curls and the backs of our ears. He knows our every thought, every moment, and every need.

However, sometimes we are like the brother to the prodigal son, right? We forget that we have access to all of heaven. We watch as other people get what they want or receive blessings and become angry or jealous of a life we don't seem to have. We are trying to do this parenting and marriage thing the right way, and we're still not getting what we want out of it! Where's our blessing?!

The hard truth is if we don't have something we need, it's because we haven't asked. We live in the Father's house. God is always near. He holds us and intimately knows us.

Remember today, just as we give our kids the world, God looks at us in heavenly places and says, "Child everything I have is yours."

RESPOND

What are a few things you need and know you have access to in God's presence?

Hope, a renewed marriage, financial blessing, healing? Write them down. Ask God for them specifically and give space for Him to respond by showing you where they are in His house.

FIFTY-ONE

If The Holy Spirit Left

"Brother Saul, the Lord Jesus, who appeared to you on the road as you came, has sent me that you may receive your sight and be filled with the Holy Spirit."
-Acts 9:17, NIV

We've been hanging out for a while together so I feel like I can shoot you straight. I'm about to ask you a tough question and I need you to answer honestly.

If the Holy Spirit left your family, would it still function the same?

Come again, Kaley? What do you mean?

I mean, are you leading as a parent by being personally influenced or spiritually inspired? Do you make all your decisions in your head or is your heart involved? Does your family stick to the basics of checking off the to-do lists, or do you ask God what's on His agenda?

What I'm really asking is this: what if our actions were an overflow of how filled our family is with the Holy Spirit? What if we let God lead in our house?

When our kids learn hard lessons from bad mistakes, we would celebrate instead of condemning them because we would know that this is God's redemptive work at play in their lives. We'd build bigger tables instead of higher fences because we'd know our neighbors well enough to invite them over for dinner. Instead of walking through marriage and motherhood in our own insecurity, we could enter into each day with confidence from Christ.

If the Holy Spirit left our life, and we could still function as normal, we are not making God our guide. So, let's function on faith today and see what freedom we find.

RESPOND

Take time to answer that question honestly. What do you think your schedule and family dynamics would look like if you truly let God guide?

What are some realistic shifts you and your family can make to let the Holy Spirit lead more in your lives?

FIFTY-TWO

Young

*"Don't let anyone look down on you because you are young,
but set an example for the believers in speech, in conduct,
in love, in faith and in purity."*
-1 Timothy 4:12, NIV

When we think of the word "young," we picture our kids. Possibly, we see some smaller version of ourselves that still eats popsicles and wears overalls.

But, really we are all constantly finding ourselves at a new beginning in life. Our marriage may still be young. We're a new mom. We just started or stopped a different job. Our kids are beginning a new year at a new school. Our newborn just transitioned into a different growth phase. There's a lot of baby steps that happen in life for all of us.

Whether we're just figuring out who God is or experiencing a shift in seasons, we don't have to let personal or family beginnings keep us from standing out.

Social media has crushed wives and moms in the "new" category. I follow a lot of mom bloggers and home designers. While a lot of their pages inspire me, they can also make me feel ashamed that I don't know how to do the things they can. I'm tossing my kids a cliff bar and slipping them into a mismatched outfit as we head out the door in the morning, and then, I see a post about a family's morning chore chart. What are morning chores!? Do people have time for this? I'm tossing my infants' disposable diapers into the trash, and I'm hit with a post about how much more resourceful cloth diapers are. "Oh no," I begin to think. "I'm killing the earth and my children. NOW WHAT!" A wife and husband post another perfectly beautiful date night picture, and I can't even remember when my spouse has seen me in anything other than sweat pants and a messy bun. I'm failing. I see a perfectly arranged living room and look up from my phone to a view of scattered goldfish, disheveled blankets, and strewn-about shoes. How do we live like this? Why can't I measure up?

I wasn't cut out for picture-perfect parenthood. Truthfully, none of us were. We're allowed to be new at caretaking or homemaking and let our best effort be enough. We can embrace a different season in motherhood and marriage with confidence in Christ who never changes. We can figure out love as we live out love. Our little faith can move big mountains.

Fresh starts are nothing to look down on. You are doing great, and God is always raising up something good.

RESPOND

What's young or new in your life and family?

Ask God what example He wants you to set in this new season. If change is causing you to worry or doubt, ask God to remind you that, no matter what, He stays constant.

FIFTY-THREE

Gratitude vs. Grumbling

*"Rejoice always, pray continually, give thanks in all circumstances;
for this is God's will for you in Christ Jesus."*
-1 Thessalonians 5:16-18, NIV

Gratitude and grumbling cannot co-exist.

I'm just going to come clean and tell you that in marriage, I choose to grumble a lot more.

I don't always tell my husband I love him, but I do always share when he forgot to wash the dishes. I don't always thank him when he takes the girls for a few hours so I can rest, but I do always tell him how tired I really am. I don't always share how much I loved our date night, but I do always put my foot down about how he hasn't helped me plan a date in a while.

Anyone else think that telling your husband about how much greener grass the grass would be on the other side if he just did X, Y, and Z is so much easier than putting in the work to cultivate the marriage we've been given? We'd rather uproot our hearts instead of sink deep into our relationship and make love grow. We tend to want more out of our spouse rather than make the most of our marriage.

Want to know the secret to contentment in marriage?

Live out your relationship as one great big thank you note to God. Stop wanting more from your spouse and start making more of the moments you have together. Be present enough to soak up the potential in the place your family is in this season. Let all your actions be a form of telling God how grateful you are He allowed you to be a safe place for another heart.

If you find yourself grumbling to your husband today, try gratitude instead. Just try it. You may find your passive-aggressive comments turn into praise, your anxiety gives way to peace, and discover some beautiful things in the broken places.

RESPOND

Do you choose gratitude or grumbling more often in your marriage?

Take time to write out a few things about your spouse you're thankful for. If you feel led, give it to them as a thank you card.

Thank you!

- -

Dear Husband,

I thank God for so much about you.
Here are just a few things I want to mention:

1.

2.

3.

4.

Sincerely,

FIFTY-FOUR

Tiny Dreamer

"Do you not realize that Christ Jesus is in you..."
-2 Corinthians 13:5, NIV

God has placed all of the answers inside of you.

I know it seems crazy, but Jesus lives within us. That means the questions we've been asking God about our purpose and placement in life actually lie within our own hearts and minds.

Think about your kids for example. From the moment they were born, they had personality, ambition, and desires. The famous question we always ask young children is, "What do you want to be when you grow up?"

They typically answer with something like the president, an astronaut, or a firefighter. It's always big and brazen. Somewhere along the way, we start believing those dreams are impossible to achieve and settle for something else. We may be Mom and Wife now. We may love it more than we would have loved being a ballerina. However, God gave us dreams. When we start to lose connection with our purpose and placement, we are ignoring our passions.

For years, I wanted to be a singer or an actress. I wanted to travel and live on a tour bus. It was going to be amazing. After taking a few steps into the music industry, I quickly realized they were going to try to change who I was so I could make them more money, be liked, and accepted. Being the type that wears her heart on her sleeve, I realized I didn't fit the bill. I can't fake much of anything (unless I'm acting), so I back peddled and kept my dreams under wraps. I was still singing for church or acting in school plays but didn't ever let myself really "go for it."

What did I lose there? What would have happened if I dared to stand my ground and put out into the world who God created me to authentically be?

What about you? What if you allowed yourself to be drawn back to who you were as a tiny dreamer with the zeal it took to take on life one bold, shaky, risky step at a time?

RESPOND

Dive as far down into your child-like mind as you'd like and answer the question: What do you want to be when you grow up?

Okay. Put your adult hat on now and answer: What do you think your God-given purpose and passion is?

What do you want your life to look like in five years? What are some realistic steps you can take to get there?

WHAT DO YOU WANT TO BE WHEN YOU GROW UP?

MY ANSWER:

WHAT DO YOU THINK YOUR GOD-GIVEN PURPOSE OR PASSION IS?

MY ANSWER:

WHAT DO YOU WANT YOUR LIFE TO LOOK LIKE IN FIVE YEARS?

MY ANSWER:

WHAT ARE SOME REALISTIC STEPS YOU CAN TAKE TO GET THERE?

MY ANSWER:

FIFTY-FIVE

The Dream Team

"Also I have given ability to all the skilled workers to make everything I have commanded you..."
-Exodus 31:6, NIV

Exodus 25-30 is basically Moses meeting with God on a mountain. Moses has just delivered the Israelite people from slavery in Egypt, and they are trying to head toward the promised land and establish what free life looks like. God decides He'd like to dwell amongst His people, so He sets up a meeting with Moses and gives him lavish instructions on how to build a tabernacle, anoint and dress priests, and make sacrifices. All of these things so that a holy God can come be present with an unholy people.

Can you imagine how overwhelmed Moses felt? God gave him a huge vision with a ton of instruction. However, it was just him on the mountain top. No team. No friends or family. No volunteers. Nothing.

But, then comes Exodus 31, and God ensures Moses he's not alone. There are specific people and skilled workers He's appointed to make this all possible.

Oftentimes, we don't follow through on what we feel like God has called us to do because we feel alone in a vision or dream. We think we can't accomplish something big because there are too many little steps to get there on our own.

What Exodus 31 shows us is our personal dreams were never meant to be accomplished personally. God might just be setting us up with a dream team waiting to join us to make it happen. All we have to do is be brave enough to share.

RESPOND

Take time today to write out a dream or goal for three different areas of your life: personal, marriage, and motherhood. Make a plan to share some of these visions with a friend, family member, or mentor. What do they think?

FIFTY–SIX

P.U.S.H

"I tell you, even though he will not get up and give you the bread because of friendship, yet because of your shameless audacity, he will surely get up and give you as much as you need."
-Luke 11:8, NIV

At my roots, I'm a good ol' Southern Baptist, and we grew up with lots of acronyms. There was the infamous W.W.J.D-What Would Jesus Do? Then, there was F.R.O.G-Fully Rely On God. However, this last one has really unfolded more in my adulthood than adolescence: P.U.S.H- Pray Until Something Happens.

P.U.S.H. is the attitude that activates our prayers. Luke 11:8 calls it "shameless audacity." In other words: perseverance, persistence, swagger, boldness. I guess the old adage "the squeaky wheel gets the grease" is a bit true in our prayer life.

We have to have enough endurance to keep praying and trust God hears and is helping us, even when we can't see it.

Before I ever met my husband, I started writing him letters. I'd feel lonely, and I'd write to let him know I missed him. I'd have questions and ask them on little slips of paper. I'd pray for him. Soon, I had started a collection box and would put items I'd gather on trips inside. A seashell from the camp I worked at on Cape Hatteras. A keychain from when I studied abroad in Belize. A rock from a mission trip in Kenya. Years and years worth of notes, prayers, and trinkets were collected before I ever encountered this mystery man.

When I was getting to know Gage, we'd talk, and I'd realize he was answering some of the questions I had written on all those papers. His character would display what I had been praying for. The more I got to know Gage, the more I realized he was the man I had been talking to the whole time. But, I possibly wouldn't have recognized him had I not been praying persistently and asking God specifically for who I thought I needed as a life partner.

If you have this book, you're probably already married. So, my point isn't to tell you how to find a husband. What I'm getting at is that persistent prayers get answered because you're expectant for God to move. You're looking at life wide-eyed because you know you're caught up in this moment, but God is playing out the long game of your life.

Like the neighbor in Luke 11 that kept knocking and relentlessly asking, we can know that if we continuously come to God, He will give us exactly what we need when we need it.

RESPOND

What persevering prayers are you tempted to give up on?

How can you find fresh inspiration for your old requests?

FIFTY-SEVEN

No Deliverance Until Development

"But he said to me, "My grace is sufficient for you, for my power is made perfect in weakness." Therefore I will boast all the more gladly about my weaknesses, so that Christ's power may rest on me."
-2 Corinthians 12:9, NIV

My husband is a student pastor and he's an expert at one-liners. Essentially, they're one-sentence-long sermons that stick with you and are perfect for rowdy teenagers who are paying more attention to their phones or the cute girl next to them than the speaker on a Sunday.

Here's one that packs a hard punch. "There's no deliverance until development."

We often think our brokenness is our fatal flaw. It's what sidelines us and makes us a bad parent, disgruntled spouse, and unworthy to be used by God,

However, our weakness is actually our strength.

Have you ever broken a bone? I have somehow climbed trees as a kid, played sports until college, and still regularly run and hike and have yet to break anything. However, I did flip a four-wheeler on my leg once. It left a gash down the top of my left thigh to my knee. To this day, I can feel how thick the scar tissue is and how hard my body worked to repair the wound.

If you've broken a bone or had any kind of serious injury, you know that when our bodies break, they rebuild stronger. Coincidentally, that's how our hearts work too.

Think about it. You're willing to offer your best advice to someone walking through something you've been through. The things that make you cry or fire you up are the places you want to change the world. Your positive passion is because of your negative experience.

So, don't just want the deliverance, desire the development. Because all the stuff you're learning through the hurt is what you'll use to heal others.

RESPOND

What do you want to be delivered from right now?

Try looking at that situation from a different angle and ask God how He's using it to develop you or your family. Write down anything that comes to mind.

FIFTY-EIGHT

The Beginning

"For the word of God is alive and active. Sharper than any double-edged sword, it penetrates even to dividing soul and spirit, joints and marrow; it judges the thoughts and attitudes of the heart."
-Hebrews 4:12, NIV

Two whole months. That's how long we've been together.

I pray you feel encouraged in your marriage, stronger in your personal faith, and empowered as a mother.

The fact you picked up this book and read it through means God has been working in your heart to become a force in your family and community. He's been sifting your soul like silt in a mining pan and pulling out the gold.

What has come to the surface?

Part of me wants to end this devotion with a good fist bump. However, I feel God telling me to share this with you: The best way to live out the three areas that most consume your life right now (matrimony, mother-hood, and me) is under the authority of God's Word. It's alive and active in your heart. It will trim away anything that doesn't belong, convict you when necessary, and always point you in the right direction. Plus, it's crammed full of promises and blessings to speak over your children and your children's children.

Remember, it's called walking with Jesus, not sprinting with Him. So, take His Guide book, His Word, and follow in lockstep with Him as you journey along. You'll always end up in the right direction.

Go change your world, radically stand committed to your spouse, and raise the next generation for Christ. God chose you for this and nothing is impossible with Him.

This isn't the end. It's just the beginning.

RESPOND

Take time to answer that question. What has risen to the surface for you from this devotional?

What is one main takeaway from "Matrimony, Motherhood, and Me" you will carry with you?

Acknowledgments:

To my husband, Gage: Thank you so much for putting up with my sporadic work hours, stubborn drive, and all together weirdness. You've always set me free to pursue my dreams and emboldened me to chase after what God has put on my heart. I wouldn't be who I am without you.

To my daughters: I hope you read this one day when you are mothers and know that, through it all, I was giving you my very best. I'm honored to raise such beautiful, powerful women and I know you're going to do great things for the Kingdom. May your children one day be as strong, sweet, and wild as you. May you pass this book down for generations to come and inspire our family to authentically love Jesus and each other.

To Amber Olafsson and the United House Publishing team: Thank you wholeheartedly for believing in me, empowering me, and challenging me. Amber, you just leaned right into what God was telling you and gave me a chance. What a joy this has been to lock arms with you all! I will never forget all this group has done for me and all young, married moms who needed a book and a team of cheerleaders to let them know they are not alone.

Notes:

1. In Touch. "The Service of Motherhood." oneplace, 2019, www.one-place.com. Accessed 20 January 2021.

2. BibleHub.com. Hupotassó. Accessed 2020. https://biblehub.com/greek/5293.htm

3. Oliver, Mary. 2019. The Uses of Sorry. Goodreads. https://www.goodreads.com/quotes/524082-the-uses-of-sorrow-in-my-sleep-i-dreamed-this.

4. Dictionary.com. n.d. self-fulfilling prophecy. WHAT DOES SELF-FULFILLING PROPHECY MEAN? Accessed 2020. https://www.dictionary.com/e/pop-culture/self-fulfilling-prophecy/.

5. Quotes.net. n.d. Quote. Dr. James Emman Kwegyir Aggrey quotes. Accessed 2020. https://www.quotes.net/quote/67261.

6. The Prayer Foundation. n.d. The Serenity Prayer. theprayerfoundation.org. Accessed 2020. https://www.prayerfoundation.org/dailyoffice/serenity_prayer_full_version.htm.

7. Chambers, Oswald. n.d. "My Utmost for His Highest." Goodreads.com. https://www.goodreads.com/quotes/6887367-april-28-what-you-will-get-thy-life-will-i.

8. Shortsleeve, Cassie. "Suicide is a Leading Cause of Death Among New Moms." InStyle, February 04, 2020. Accessed April 16, 2020. https://www.instyle.com/beauty/health-fitness/maternal-suicide-postpartum-depression.

About the Author

Kaley Rivera Thompson is an author, copywriter, and worship leader. Her passion to see women love God and each other authentically has led her to lead worship for ministries across the greater Charlotte area and design devotional books for over a decade. When she's not writing or playing her guitar, Kaley loves to sip strong coffee, go on hikes, or take a day trip to the mountains with her family. She is the wife to TWELVE sports ministry leader, Gage Thompson and mom to two little girls, Lina and Lili.

You can follow her on instagram at @kriverathompson.

CPSIA information can be obtained
at www.ICGtesting.com
Printed in the USA
BVHW091226021121
620551BV00012B/1082/J